MAKING DECORATIONS

Elizabeth Gundrey is the author of four other Piccolo books, *Sewing Things*, *Growing Things*, *Make Your Own Monster* and *Collecting Things*; and of *Fun With Art*, *Fun Food*, *Fun and Flowers* and *Fun Dressing-up* (all for children). She has written many family books such as *Go-as-you-please Holidays*, *Your Money's Worth* and *At Your Service*. She used to edit *Shopper's Guide* and she writes articles for newspapers.

By the same author in Piccolo

Sewing Things
Growing Things
Make Your Own Monster
Collecting Things

MAKING DECORATIONS

for birthday parties, Christmas and other special occasions

Written and Designed by
ELIZABETH GUNDREY

Cover by David Davies
Text Illustrations by Robin Lawrie

A Piccolo Original

PAN BOOKS LTD
LONDON AND SYDNEY

First published 1973 by Pan Books Ltd,
Cavaye Place, London SW10 9PG

ISBN 0 330 23753 5

2nd Printing 1974

To Frieda

*Printed in Great Britain by
Cox & Wyman Ltd, London, Reading and Fakenham*

Contents

There are lots of days in the year worth a celebration. Christmas, birthdays, Easter, New Year – whenever you have a party. Your parents' wedding anniversary, christenings, confirmation day or a barmitzvah. What about Hallowe'en and Guy Fawkes' day? Or your favourite saint's day? And the day when you celebrate passing an exam, winning a prize or helping the school team to victory!

Here are dozens of ways to decorate your rooms for special occasions like these.

Golden Rules

1. Keep paper and plastic decorations away from fires, candles or lights – they might go up in flames. Never leave candles alight when you're not in the room. Night-lights are safer.

2. Choose one or two colours and stick to these within one room. Too much of a mixture looks a mess.

3. When using paint or glue, spread *lots* of newspaper around to catch drips.

4. Keep large plastic bags away from your younger brothers and sisters, who could be suffocated if they put them over their heads.

Collect and Buy

Find a big box, and start collecting now. Collect any bits and pieces that look pretty – they'll all come in useful sometime. Odd bits of coloured string or ribbon or lace. Foil bottle-tops and wrappings. Old beads and bits of broken jewellery. Any and every kind of cardboard. Patterned paper and bags, and leftover pieces of wallpaper.

Modelling materials like clay and Plasticine will be very handy (you can make a useful modelling dough yourself from a pound of flour, 2 oz salt and some water, which will be good enough for most purposes in this book).

So will all kinds of glue and other sticking substances. One that you can make yourself is: 2 tablespoons Polycell in an old plastic squeezy-bottle, filled up with water. This is strong enough for simple paper-and-paste sticking.

Here is a list of lots more things that are useful to have.

Kitchen foil, foil patty-pans, silver paper.

Paper doilies, especially gold or silver ones.

Drinking straws, especially coloured ones.

Plastic beads (looking like coloured glass ones), sold by toyshops.

Felt-tip pen, big, black.

Picture-pins to fasten things to walls or ceilings – they don't make nasty marks and are stronger than drawing-pins. (Sold by ironmongers.)

Glitter-powder (gold and silver), or artificial snow.

Cardboard

Cotton wool for snow etc.

Invisible thread (sold by needlework shops) for hanging things up.

Copydex adhesive. You can stick almost anything with this, it's very clean, and you can simply rub it off if you want to remove it.

Clear glue (like Sellobond) for jobs where more strength is needed, or to use on transparent or shiny things.

'*Everlasting flowers*' (*helichrysums*) and other dried flowers which keep their shape without being in water.

Gold and silver paint in aerosol sprays to transfigure all sorts of things – from eggs and sea-shells to feathers and ferns.

Coloured papers – tissue, crêpe, patterned wrapping-paper, bright wallpapers, Cellophane.

Gold cord, coloured string, ribbon, bits of lace, etc.

Blu-Tack, which is a rubbery substance, useful for sticking things on walls. It leaves no mark.

Double-sided Sellotape (both surfaces are sticky), or 'magic mounts' – for fastening things onto woodwork, etc. You can peel them off afterwards.

Wire, both the springy and bendy kinds. Thin springy wires are sold by florists, ordinary bendy wire by ironmongers.

Wall Decorations

Walls are nice big spaces to hang decorations on. Don't damage them though, when you fix things up. Page 11 lists fixing methods that are harmless.

Pennants and Streamers

For these you will need strips of coloured paper or fabric 6″ wide and 1 yd long. Crêpe paper is suitable. You can decorate your strips in any of the ways shown – or invent your own ideas. Hang them with 2 picture-pins at the top, or with a good lump of Blu-Tack.

No. 1. has a bow of silvery kitchen-foil (3″ wide) at the top, 6″ foil letters down it and a foil fringe at the bottom. For a birthday party, these could spell the name of the child. Stick them on with Copydex.

No. 2. is decorated with gold string (sold for tying Christmas parcels), 6″ bells cut out of gold paper, and an 18″ strip of gold paper (3″ wide) cut out and pleated like this to go at the top:

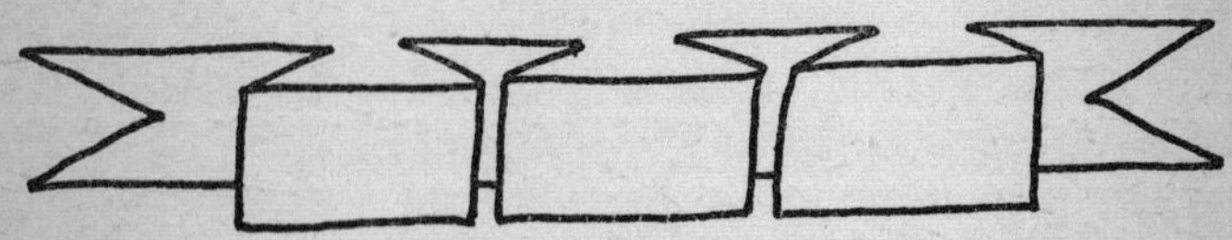

NOEL

For Christmas the streamer could be red. For your parents' wedding anniversary, white. To stick the string on, squeeze a trail of clear glue from the tube onto the paper and press the string onto it. Glue silver sequins, or glass-like plastic beads, onto the bells – you could use beads from a broken string of 'pearls', or some other broken necklace.

No. 3. has holly and ivy pushed into a small ball of crumpled chicken wire, safety-pinned to a felt pennant. (Cut the wire with pliers, bending the sharp edges away from your hands.) Instead of the leaves you could use paper flowers – see page 92 – or a bunch of baubles.

How to Make a Swag

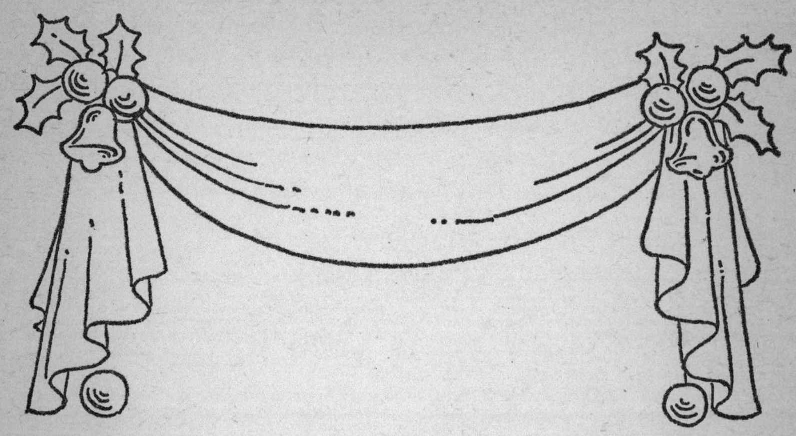

Cut this out of coloured tissue or, better still, out of muslin, or plastic bags from the dry-cleaners, to be sprayed gold when complete. Put it over a mirror, a fireplace, your collection of greetings cards, the poster on p. 18 or even at the head of your bed. Make it whatever size you need, depending on where you plan to hang it.

The centre piece starts like this:

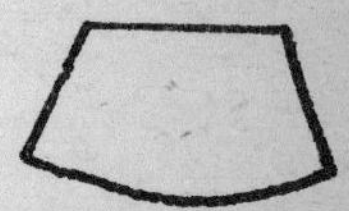

Gather as shown, and hold with pins or Copydex.

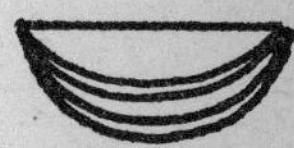

Fasten the swag to the wall with picture-pins, and then cover the joins with baubles and holly.

The two 'tails' are this shape before gathering and sticking to the ends of the centre piece:

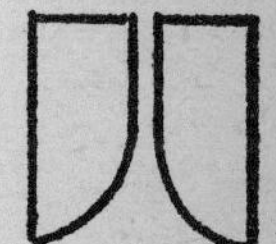

A Wall Vase

You need a waterproof container, such as a small plastic box. Cut a piece of felt or other firm fabric, straight on top and curved below, big enough to go round the box and hold it close to the wall.* Tap picture-pins in to hold it at the upper corners and below where the box will go. With the box in place, pour water in then arrange the flowers or, for Christmas, holly, ivy and tinsel.

You could use an old straw hat with the brim folded back at the top, and long ribbons tied round it.

*For a box 5″×4″×2″ you might need a piece of fabric 9″×18″ from which to cut the semi-circle.

Golden Trumpets

Each trumpet needs a piece of cardboard about 2′ by 6″, covered with gold paper. Draw the trumpet shape on the back of one (the stem should be 1½″ wide), cut out and use it as a guide to draw the shape on the back of the second card. Cut this out, too. Use a black felt-tip pen to draw in details.

Glue a few matchboxes to the backs of the trumpets where they will not show, crossing the trumpets as shown in the picture, so they will not be flat against the wall.

Put Blu-Tack or magic mounts on the other sides of the matchboxes, and press these against the wall. Where the trumpets cross, fasten some evergreens, baubles, etc (use Sellotape).

An Outsize Poster

Here's one which can be made by all the family, and friends. Get each person to paint, draw or cut out in coloured tissue one of the gifts from the carol 'The Twelve Days of Christmas'. Each should be stuck onto a piece of paper of the same size – 8″×12″ would do. You could use plain white cartridge paper, but the effect would be gayer if you bought a scrapbook with different coloured papers inside and cut the pages out.

When all the drawings and collages are done, lay them out in the right order on a large table or a smooth floor and, with the help of a friend to hold them, join them together with long strips of coloured Sellotape – the metallic kind would look festive, or add glue and glitter-powder. Put a border of Sellotape round the four sides too. (You will need about 30′ of tape).

Here are the twelve gifts named in the carol: A partridge in a pear tree, two turtle doves, three French hens, four calling birds, five gold rings, six geese laying, seven swans swimming, eight maids milking, nine ladies dancing, ten lords leaping, eleven pipers piping, twelve drummers drumming.

Pleated Angels

Cut from white paper, these look lovely on a coloured wall. Use double-sided Sellotape or Blu-Tack to fix them. Take a piece of white paper, draw a circle round a small plate, and cut out. Cut the circle in three places as shown – be sure not to cut right into the middle. (To find where the cuts should go, you could fold the circle in half, then in half again, and use the creases as a guide.)

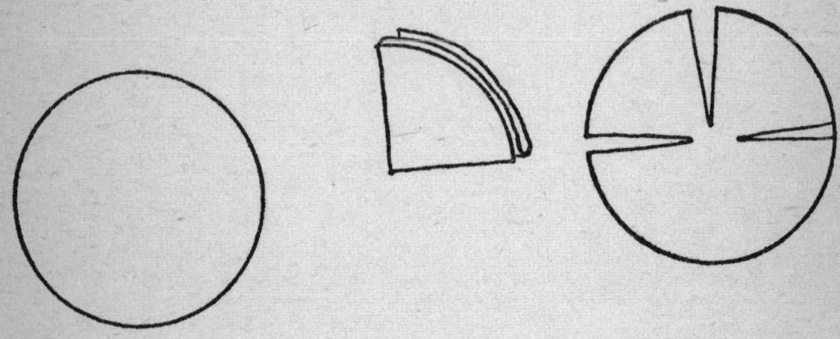

Now pleat each of the three segments with your fingers (taking care not to tear the middle). You now have the angel's wings and skirt. See opposite.

On a piece of paper about 3″×2″ draw the outline of head, chest and arms using the shapes shown opposite. Cut out and stick (with Copydex) to the front of the angel.

Stick a halo behind the angel's head – use a 1″ circle of gold paper, or paper with glitter-powder glued on. Glue between her hands a tiny spray of dried flowers or a very small Christmas-tree bauble with some tinsel.

Think of other figures to make like this – Columbine, fairies, etc.

Decorative Plaques

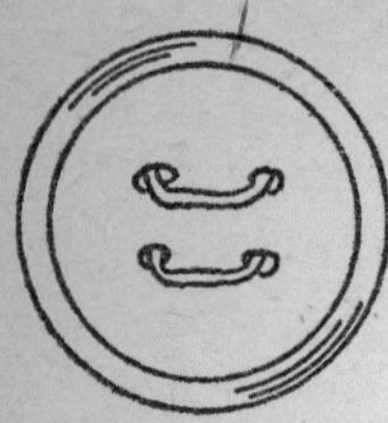

For these, use shallow foil dishes (the sort used for pies), or cover round cheese-boxes or paper plates with kitchen foil, or spray them with gold paint. With a skewer or sharp knitting-needle poke four small holes in the centre of the dish, and thread two wire loops through, fastening them securely at the back (see above). You can now use these loops to hold whatever decoration you want to put in each plaque. Here are some ideas:

a posy of 'everlasting' flowers (you can buy these in most florists – two good varieties are *statice* and *helichrysum*).

a bunch of tiny Christmas-tree baubles, with a bow made from ribbon or crêpe paper

a sprig of holly, or heather

dried seed-heads from the garden, painted with poster-paints

paper flowers (see page 92)

The plaque can be hung on picture-pins, using the wires at the back.

Candle Bracket

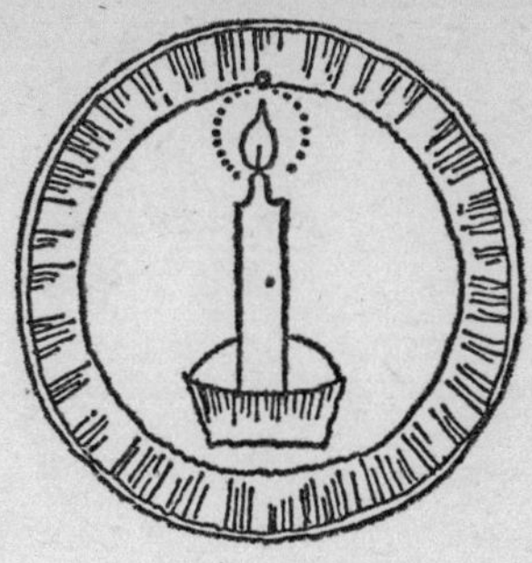

Candle flames will seem twice as bright when reflected in the foil.

Cover a paper plate with foil, or use a foil pie-plate. Cut a foil patty pan like this:

and bend the back part upwards. Fix this to the foil plate, using Sellotape.

Now stand a short candle in the pan, using a little melted wax from it to fix it securely. This decoration is quite safe but be careful to blow the candle out before you leave the room.

Wall Trees

If you aren't going to have a real Christmas tree this year, here are two alternatives.

Buy green crêpe paper and cut it into strips a foot wide. Fold these in half longways, and snip as shown:

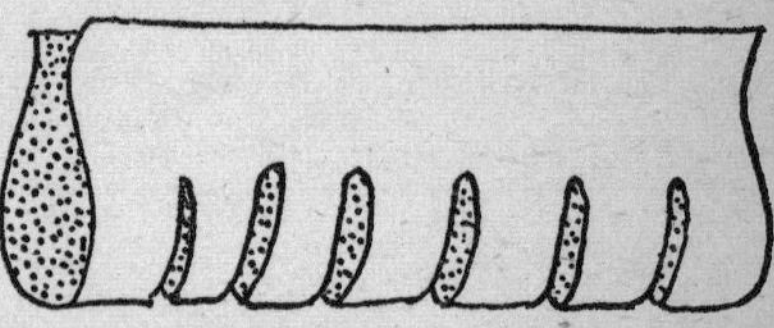

Turn inside out and glue the top edges together. Glue them by their tops onto a sheet of newspaper. Start at the bottom with a length of about 2′. About 4″ above this, glue down another length – about 2″ shorter. Keep on doing this, overlapping each layer, until you reach the top of the newspaper. Cut off the surplus newspaper.

On another piece of newspaper, glue down strips of coloured paper in a tub shape.

Fix these to the wall with double-sided Sellotape or Blu-Tack, and decorate the tree by pinning on a star (at the top), tinsel, etc – use only lightweight things. You can curve the bottom of the tree to give a three-dimensional look.

Another tree:

Buy the largest piece of green card that you can get. Art shops sell it. Pencil a tree outline on it – keep it very simple – then cut out.

Tack tinsel in festoons from side to side as shown. Either use a stapler to fasten it at the sides of the tree, or bits of Sellotape. Add baubles at the points and in any spaces. Put a star at the top.

You could put glue and glitter-powder all round the edges.

Fix to the wall with magic mounts, or with picture-pins.

A Big Winter Bouquet

For this you need one polystyrene ceiling tile (sold by paint and wallpaper shops), a packet of small gold doilies, some foil patty-pans and either everlasting flowers from a florist or little home-made paper ones – see page 92.

Cut the corners off the tile and make it roughly round in shape. Cover it with patty-pans pinned to it through the doilies: put the pins in at an angle. Pull the doilies forward, not flat, so that they are crowded into the space available.

Glue one of the flowers in the middle of each pan. When the tile is full of flowers, make a big bow of crêpe paper and pin or Copydex it at the bottom.

A loop of tape at the back of the tile can be glued on and used to hang the bouquet on the wall. Although big, it is very light.

Joy Bells

For these you need felt or some other firm fabric (red and white), gold braid, which you can buy in the haberdashery or lampshade departments of most big stores – and a little gold Christmas-tree bauble for each bell. Buy the gold braid in two widths – one almost like string, and the other a bit wider. For each bell, if you made it about 9″ long, you would need approximately: 6″×7″ red fabric, 6″×2½″ white fabric and ⅔ yard each of the two braids.

Cut the red shape like this and the white like this . Stick the red shape above the white on backing paper. Trim with gold braid as shown, and pin or stitch the gold bauble into place.

Use Blu-Tack or double-sided Sellotape to fix the bells in place on the wall.

Filigree Frames

Put a silver frame behind a favourite greetings card, a little mirror, the candle-bracket on page 23, or the plaques on page 22, and they will look more important and more festive too.

Lay a sheet of foil on a sheet of newspaper and, using a very big plate as a guide, cut out a circle from both. Cut the newspaper circle in half, and then fold the foil in half over it. From the leftover paper, cut a quarter circle, and fold the foil again over it. Finally, cut a $\frac{1}{8}$ circle from the paper and fold the foil over this.

PAPER

FOIL

Round the edge, snip out various shapes:

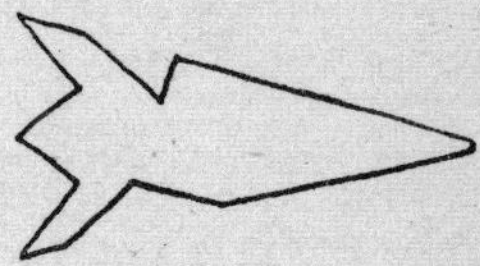

Unfold, remove the newspaper, and you will have a decorative background on which to place a plaque, circular picture, etc before hanging it.

A Flying Angel

This one should be about 2′ across and has eight parts which you cut out of newspaper. First, cut out the head and body, snip the bottom of the tunic and pull slightly forward. Then the arms, stick one at the back and one in front; tuck a bit of cotton wool or paper under the front arm so that it stands out; glue fingertips together. Next the halo: it goes behind the head, with a bit of cotton wool between. Then the overskirt: cut some V-shapes and pull forward. Finally, the petticoat and wings: pleat with fingers before sticking behind. The wings are ¼-circles of paper. After you have glued these together put them on more sheets of newspaper before spraying gold on. When dry, fix to the wall with double-sided Sellotape, Blu-Tack or dabs of Copydex.

Why not make a pair, facing one another?

Clowns

Hang a row of paper plates round the room, each painted with a different clown face. Use poster paints and put it on nice and thick. To hang, pierce two small holes at the top and thread red cord through.

The Three Kings

On a sheet of coloured paper about 2′ by 1½′, do a paper collage. Leave the top 2″ blank to turn over a long stick or rod, by which to hang it up. Glue another stick at the bottom: this will pull the paper straight. Do any subject you like (or copy this one).

Keep the outlines simple. Draw them first on plain paper, then cut out each shape and use it for a pattern when cutting out the coloured papers to stick down.

Look for some wrapping papers with small patterns, stripes, etc, on them. Add coloured string, wool, small buttons and beads for decoration, and make a strip of paper fringe to go along the bottom.

You could add glue and glitter-powder to crowns and fringes.

Paper Plaits

Cut three strips of crêpe paper about 2′ long and 2″ wide. With a safety-pin, fasten the three ends together on a chair-arm or seat and firmly pull the opposite ends – the strips will stretch taut. Keeping them pulled straight, plait the strips together. Remove the safety-pin, and secure the ends with Sellotape wound round, about 2″ long.

Now curve the plait round and Sellotape it into a circle with the ends on top. Pull the ends out to make a pretty bow as in the picture, and decorate with touches of glitter-powder or gold spray.

Attach to the wall and hang a silver bauble (use invisible thread) so that it is suspended right in the middle of the circle.

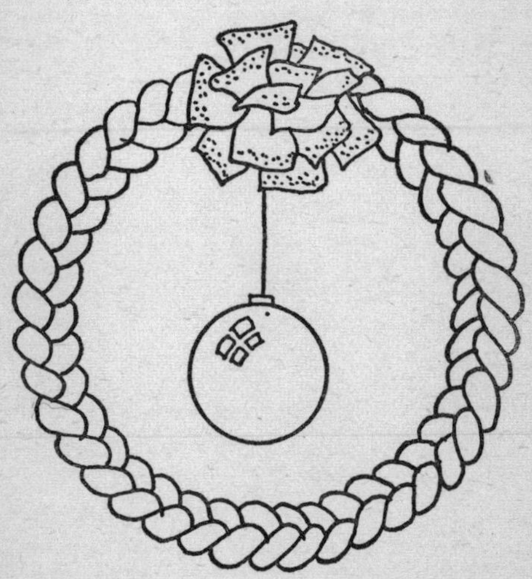

Santa's Balloon

Use chocolate papers, parcel wrappings, ribbons and gold string to make this easy and effective wall decoration. Instead of doing Santa, you could try all sorts of other figures: there are some ideas at the end of the instructions.

Pencil onto cardboard the shapes for the balloon, the basket and Santa. Cut out diamond-shapes from foil chocolate wrappings and stick on the balloon (add a few beads if you like). Use a scrap of parcel wrapping-paper to cover the basket, and some red paper or paint plus cotton wool to make Santa. Glue him to the basket. Join the basket to the balloon with gold cords. Fasten on the wall with double-sided Sellotape, or Blu-Tack.

Other ideas: a sledge full of parcels, Good King Wenceslas, carol singers, a circus, Harlequin.

Window Decorations

Hang decorations where they can be seen from outdoors as well as in. Choose materials that show up well against the light.

Snow Scene

Pull a chunk of cotton wool into small bits. Thread a needle with a length of 'invisible' sewing-thread – it should be as long as the window where you are going to hang it. String the cotton-wool snowflakes onto this, about 3″ apart. Do as many threads as you need to fill the window, pinning them (or sticking them with tiny pieces of Sellotape or Blu-Tack) to hang from the top of its frame. Paint a robin on cardboard (or cut one from a Christmas card) and add this, or anything else you like, with cotton-wool snow, to the window sill.

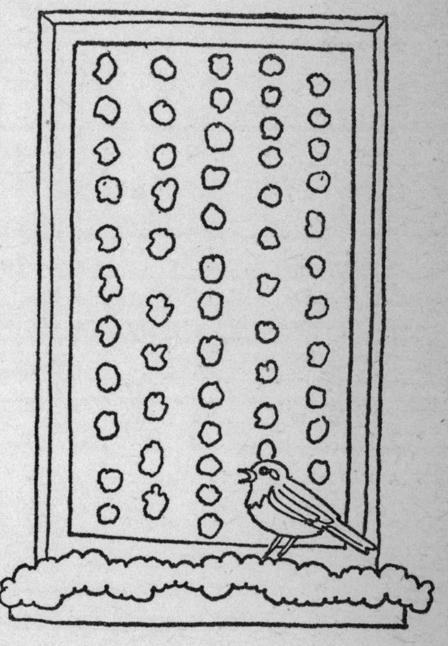

Tissue Banners

Take a sheet of light-coloured tissue paper, 20″×30″, and fold it in sixteen. That is, fold it in half four times. Then cut out shapes round its edges – squares, triangles, semicircles etc. Unfold, and with Sellotape at the top, fasten it to the top of the window.

If the window has lots of small panes, you could make small banners – a different colour for each pane.

You could also make matching table mats. Cover the tissue with transparent Fablon or Con-Tact on both sides. If you like, add a few sequins, dried leaves, etc, between the tissue and the top layer of Fablon.

Silver Bauble

You can make this enormous if you like, just by using lots more patty-pans. Here are instructions for a small one, using eight small, shallow foil patty-pans. (You could make three baubles to hang on one string.)

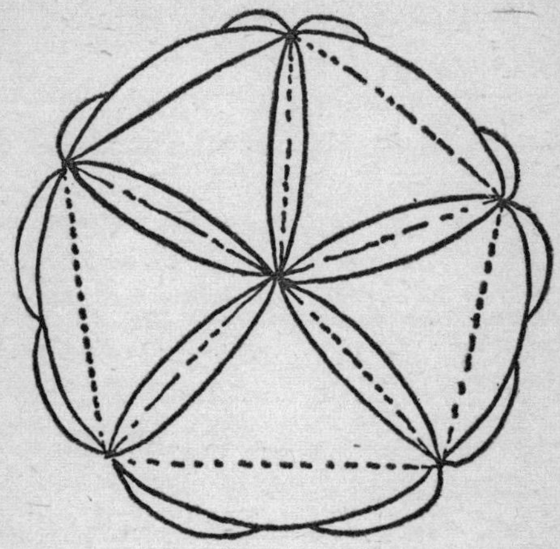

Bend the edges of each pan upwards to make a triangle shape in the bottom:

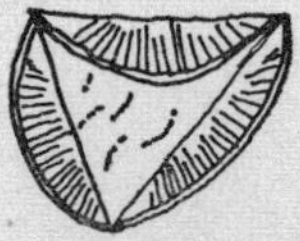

Fasten one side of one pan to one side of another. (The easiest way is with a paper-stapler, though you could use glue or Sellotape.) Keep on doing this until every side is fastened to another pan. The pans will automatically curve round into a ball shape. Make a hole through which to thread a coloured cord, and hang up in the window to reflect the light as the bauble sways.

Stars

Paper and straw

1.

Fold a doily (white, silver or gold) in eight and cut as shown. Open out and stick on window with a dab of Copydex in the middle. Do lots of them.

2.

Press eight coloured, transparent drinking straws onto a drawing-pin as shown. Make a knot at the end of a long piece of gold cord and wind it three times round the middle of the star, going over and under the straws alternately. Tie a knot at the back, remove the drawing-pin and hang the star up.

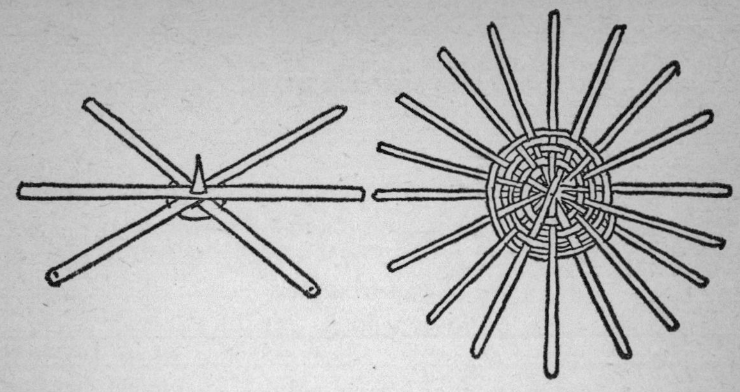

3.

Glue together six coloured, transparent drinking straws as in the diagram. When firmly set, hang a Christmas-tree bauble in the middle, and then hang the star in the window. Transparent sewing-thread is ideal for this.

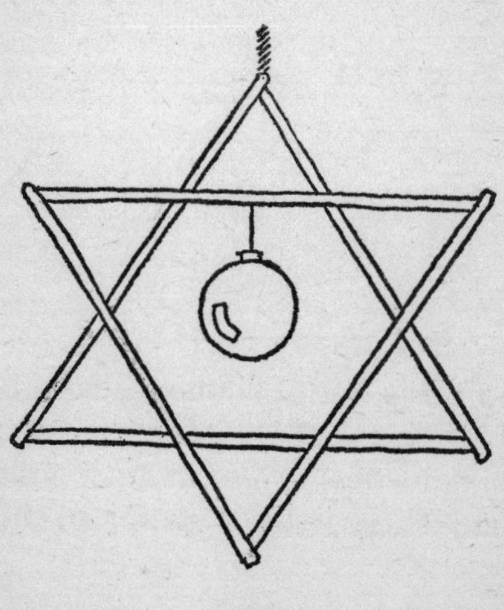

More Stars

Transparent and silvery

4.

From a sheet of coloured, transparent self-adhesive plastic cut some 5″ squares (leave the backing-paper on). Fold each square in four (half and half again), then fold in half diagonally so that you have a triangle.

Holding it with the folded edges on the right and along the bottom, cut across to a point half way down the left edge, then cut from there to a point half way along the bottom edge. Open out, peel off the backing-paper and stick to the window.

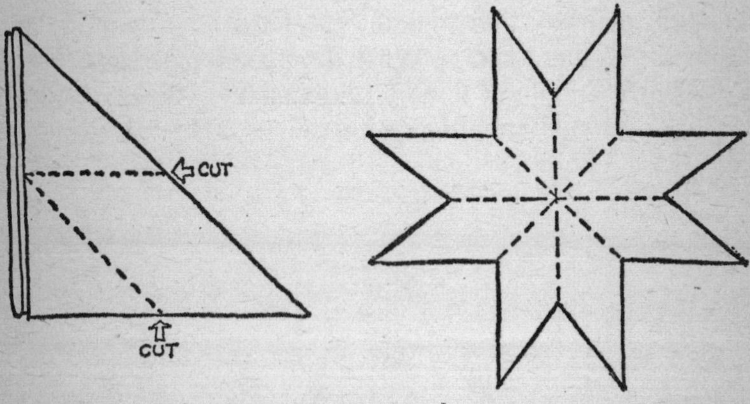

5.

Cut five-pointed stars out of shallow silver-foil patty-pans and, bending their points slightly forward, stick them onto the window with dabs of Copydex in the middle. Or, making them slightly smaller, stick them on top of the transparent stars.

6.

Cut a foil patty-pan into eight segments. In a small, raw potato (or a ball of Plasticine), cut a number of deep slits and push into them the broad ends of the foil segments (see diagram). The potato should be completely covered. Make a hole through it with a skewer and push a piece of wire through. You can hang your star from the pelmet.

The Kissing-Ring

Cut two or three strips of coloured card 2′–3′ long and about 1″–2″ wide. Decorate them with painted patterns, coloured Sellotape or gold spray. Glue the ends of each, to make a ring. Put the rings inside one another, then pierce holes at top and bottom (where the rings cross one another). Thread a long gold or coloured cord through, making a knot underneath the tops of the rings. Leave a 'tail' at the bottom onto which to tie a sprig of mistletoe.

Or you could make a crown shape:

Pretty Parsley

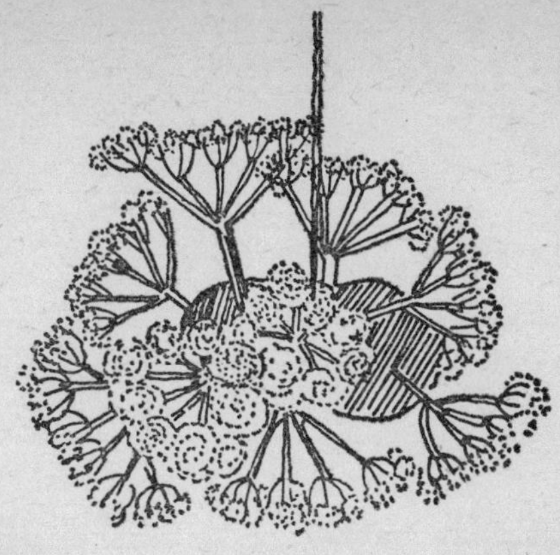

In autumn fields and hedgerows you will find, stiff and dry, the dead but very pretty stems of cow parsley and its relatives – hogweed, chervil, ground elder, wild carrot and parsnip, etc. All of them have 'umbrellas' of tiny seeds on fine stalks which grow from bigger stems like this:

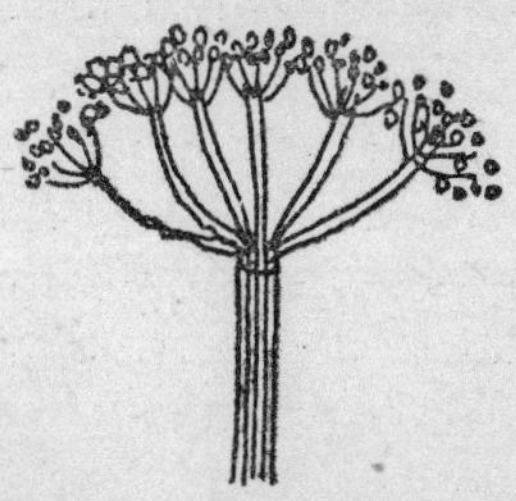

Collect lots of these, and cut them to about 6″ long. In a fairly small, round potato make a lot of holes with a skewer, and push the stiff parsley stalks in – stick a nail into the top of the potato and tie a cord to it to hang up your parsley ball. Spray it first with gold or silver paint.

(Instead of parsley, you could use dried hydrangea flower-heads from the garden.)

Tassels

You could hang a golden tassel at the bottom of many of the decorations in the book. To make one, take a strip of gold paper and snip it like this:

Then roll it up, fix the end with glue, and pull the ends out slightly:

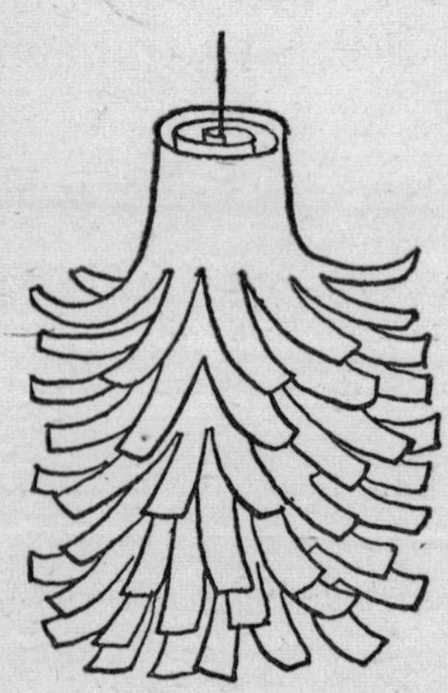

You can pull the centre ones down a long way.

Holly Berries

If you want to add a sprig of holly to a decoration but it has no berries, light a red candle and hold it pointing downwards over a cup of cold water. Most of the drops that fall off will be nice and round.

Slightly warm the holly leaves (in a warm oven or over a radiator – just for a few minutes) and lift the wax drops (on the tip of a pointed kitchen knife) onto the leaves. As the leaves are warm, the wax drops will stick.

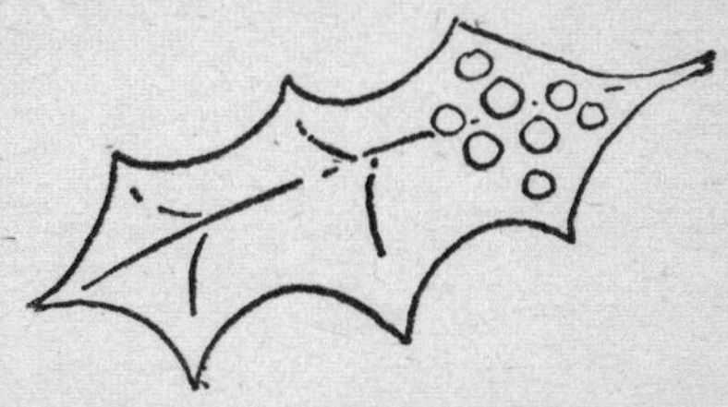

Cellophane Pictures

Coloured Cellophane (or tissue) can be stuck to glass windows with a clear glue like Sellobond (you need put on only very tiny dabs). When you want to remove it, nail varnish remover or acetone will get it off.

With it use coloured Sellotape, particularly the pretty metallic kind. This simply peels off when you want to remove it.

The light will shine through the Cellophane but not the Sellotape.

If you want black lines, use a thick black felt-tip pen.

Keep the shapes simple. And remember that, when using coloured Cellophane, if you put one colour on top of another you create a new colour. Yellow on red makes orange. Red on blue makes purple. Blue on yellow makes green.

Here are some ideas for Cellophane pictures using very simple shapes.

A Stripy Candle
Short lengths of coloured Cellophane overlapping one another. Flame made from yellow over red Cellophane. Do a row of them.

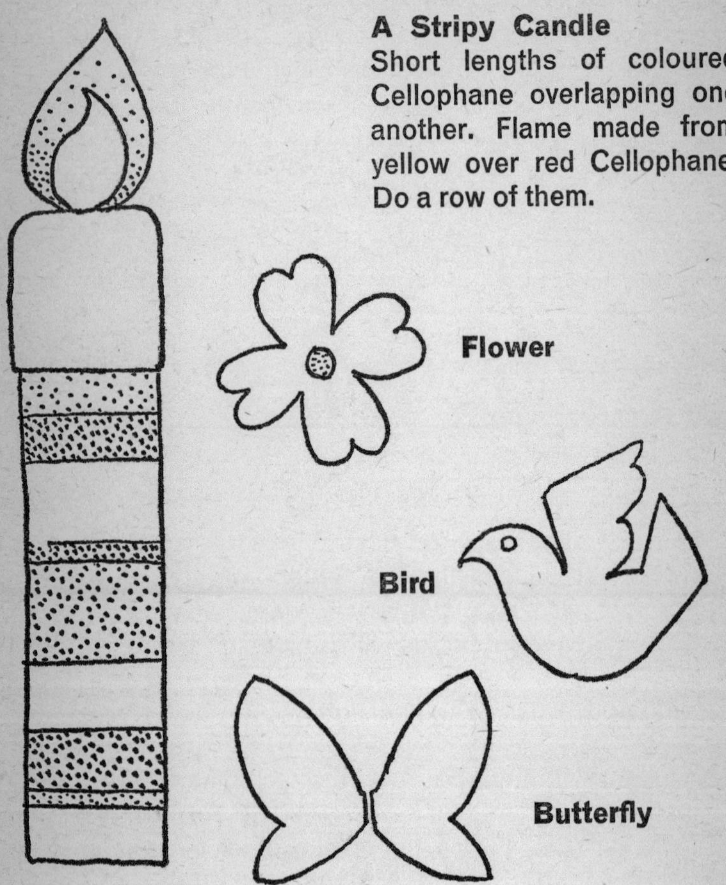

Bunch of Balloons
Coloured Cellophane with letters of metallic Sellotape. Strings drawn directly onto the window with black felt-tip pen.

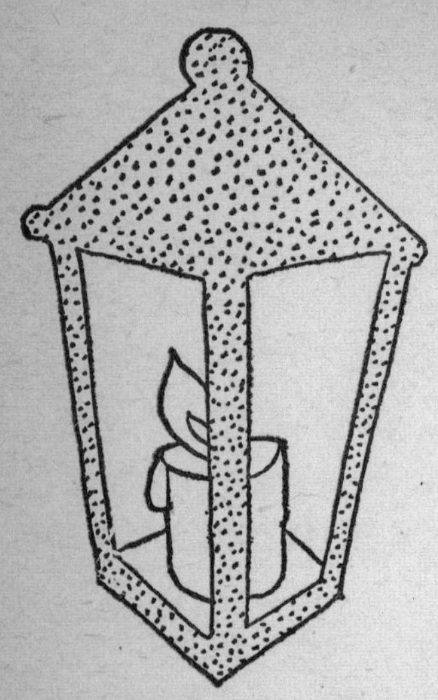

A Lantern
Metallic Sellotape for the lantern, red Cellophane for the candle, yellow Cellophane for the flame.

A Cracker
Yellow Cellophane (in the middle) on top of red. Scatter them all over the window.

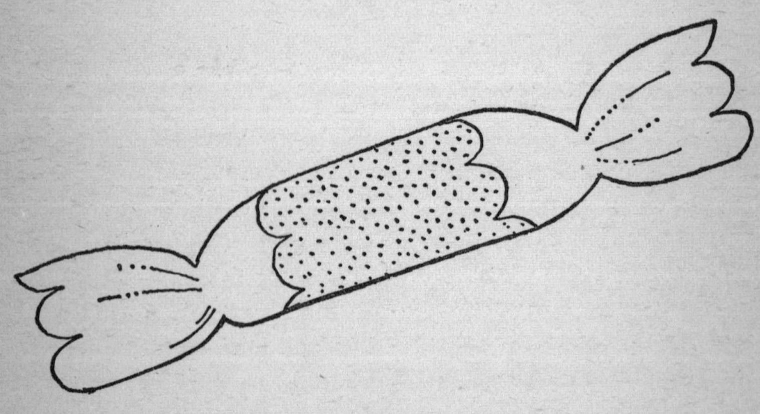

Swaying Rings

Cut out a circle of white paper about 4″ across. Fold in half, and cut round inside it about ½″ – then cut again, ½″ – and again.

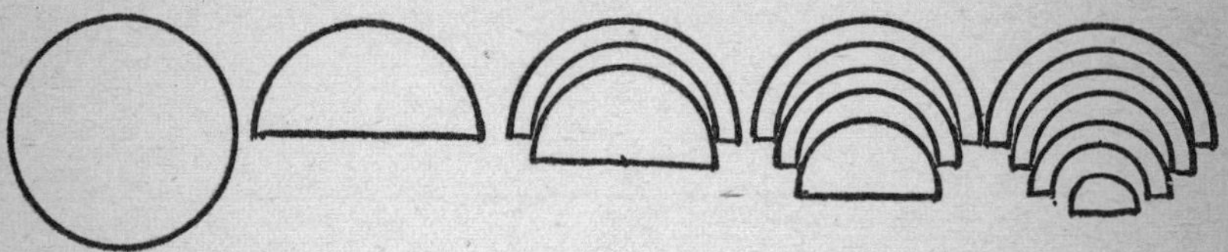

Throw away the middle bit and open out the remaining three rings. Glue together like this:

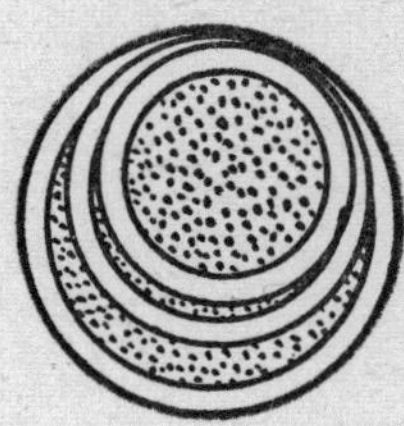

At the back, glue to the biggest ring a piece of coloured Cellophane (or tissue) and trim it to fit.

Make a lot of these and hang them up against the window on invisible sewing-threads of different lengths, so that the light will shine through.

Invent other shapes for this purpose – triangles, butterflies, flowers, diamonds, etc. Try using Cellophane in two colours. Foil rings are even prettier than paper ones, but put a piece of paper between the folded foil before cutting, to keep it from sticking together.

Swinging Snowman

Tear a newspaper into strips.

Take a blown-up balloon, perch it on a bowl on the draining-board, and paste the strips on, about three layers thick. You can make paste from 2 oz flour and ½ cup water or buy wallpaper paste. Don't cover the knot on the balloon. Finish with layers of white tissue, Kleenex or kitchen paper. Leave overnight to dry in a warm place, then paint on eyes, nose and mouth, *keeping the knot at the top*. Cut a hat from black paper, roughly like this:

Bend round and glue

Push down over crown and stick

Cut a red scarf from crêpe paper, knot it round his neck, fixing it with Copydex. Hang up by the knot, or stand him on a cardboard ring. Do a Humpty-Dumpty for Easter.

Pompoms

Cut eight circles from Cellophane (or tissue), about 4″ across. Fold them in four – do each one separately. Take a darning needle and wool, and thread each circle onto the wool – the needle should go through the corner.

When all eight are on the wool, tie the wool ends securely but do NOT pull tight; and leave the tail hanging.
Pull the circles out very gently, and hang a cluster of pompoms at the window, by their wool tails.

More Balloon Ideas

(Think out the colour scheme before you start.)

Posy Balloon

Cut four strips of coloured tissue, 2′×3″, and glue their tops and bottoms together. Hang up with a balloon at the bottom, round end downwards. Pinch each tissue 'ribbon' together about half way up, and fasten with gold Sellotape. Cut a gold paper doily into strips and fix (with Copydex) to the balloon between the ribbons. At the top of this, fix small paper flowers. Using Sellotape, fasten a big paper flower or bow to the top of the balloon, and a gold paper tassel below. (Paper flowers: see p. 92 Tassels: p. 44). To make a Sellotape bow, first stick two lengths together, enclosing their sticky sides.

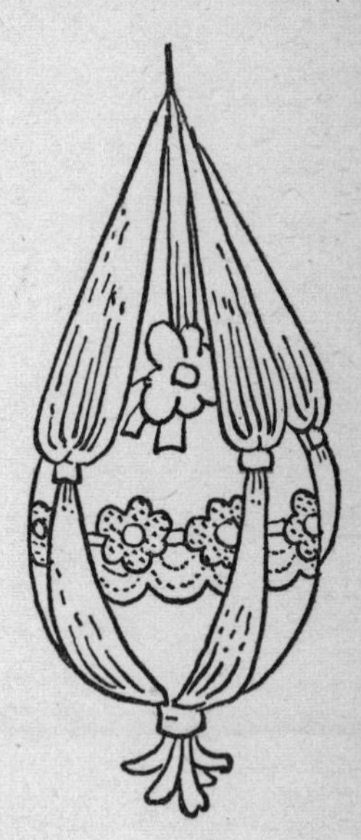

Butterfly Balloon

Cover a balloon with kitchen foil, just press it on. Using coloured metallic Sellotape for the bodies, fasten on wings cut from 6″ squares of Cellophane and tissue of different colours. Each wing should have tissue under Cellophane, with the Cellophane ½″ higher than the tissue. Bend the wings up slightly. Draw antennae with black felt-tip pen.

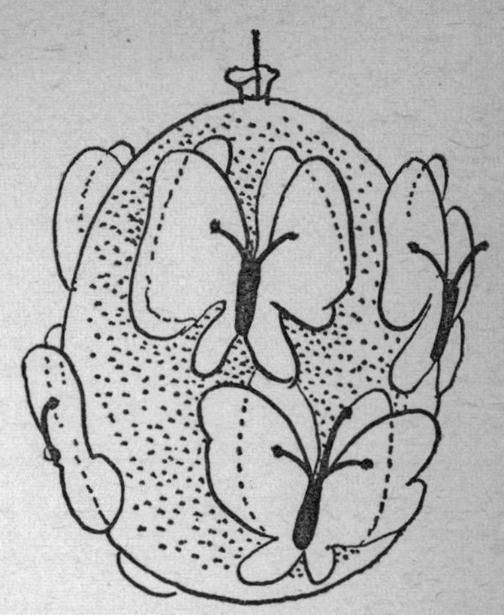

Hula Balloon

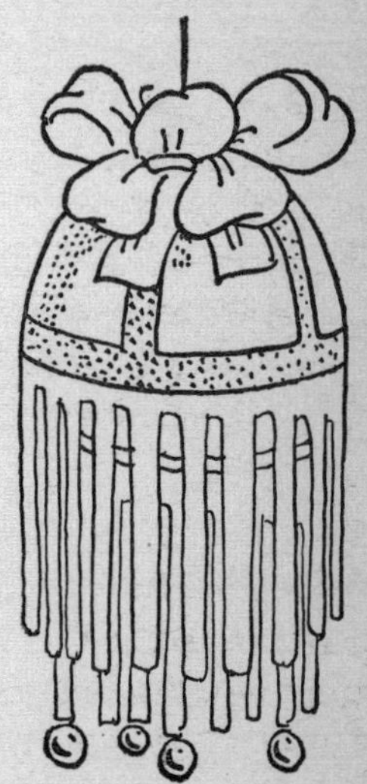

Fold up a 2′ long piece of tissue to cut it into strips 1½′ long – don't cut right to the top. Unfold and fasten round the middle of the balloon with metallic Sellotape. Put another 'skirt' (1½′ long) on, below and beneath this one. Add a few very tiny baubles to some of the ends. Use more metallic tape on the upper half of the balloon, making a bow at the top.

Monster Easter Egg

First make a giant egg cup for which you need to buy some 12″ chicken wire. You will need about 2′. Bend it round into a cylinder, then squeeze the middle in until you have made an egg-cup shape. Cover this with strips of paper and paste (see p. 50), dry for a day or so and then paint. Put a white balloon in (rounded end upwards) for the egg. Cut an outsize spoon from cardboard to go with it – and put it at Dad's place on the breakfast table for an outsize surprise!

Fireplace Decorations

The fireplace is often the most important part of a room. So dress it up for special occasions. But *don't* work on it while the fire is alight.

If you put paper decorations above an open fire, be sure it is covered by a fireguard, just in case they fall.

Mantelpiece Edgings

Tissue

The quickest way to dress up the edge of the mantelpiece is to cut a strip of coloured tissue 4″ wide and as long as the mantelpiece (you will probably have to put several strips together). Fold the strip up like this:

Cut out a simple shape (it must leave the sides still uncut at one or two points).

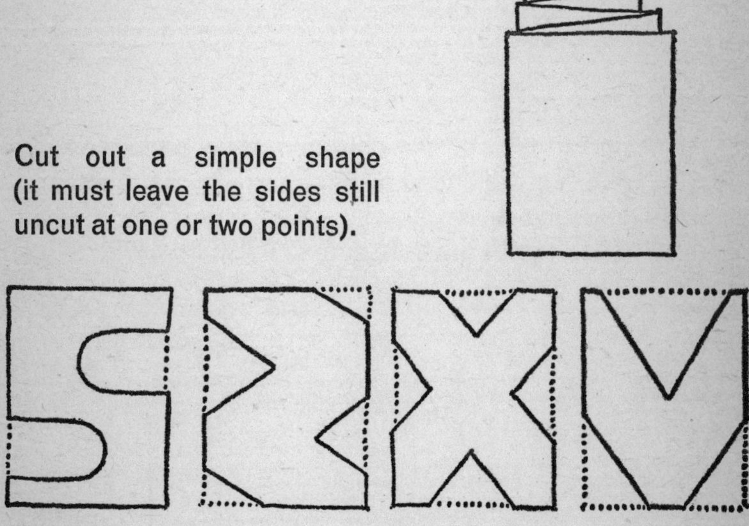

When you undo the strip, you can stick it to the edge of the mantelpiece with two or three dabs of Copydex.
You could make two strips in different colours and designs and put one on top of the other.

Pleated

For a pleated trimming, use coloured shiny paper cut into strips 1″ wide. You will need two colours – perhaps red and gold (or gold and silver, or silver and blue). Lay the red strip on the table with the gold across it like this, with a dab of glue to fix them:

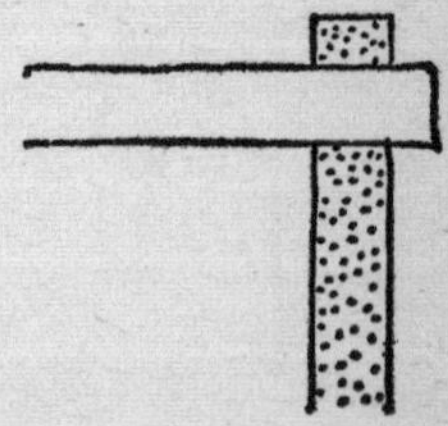

Fold the red strip upwards:

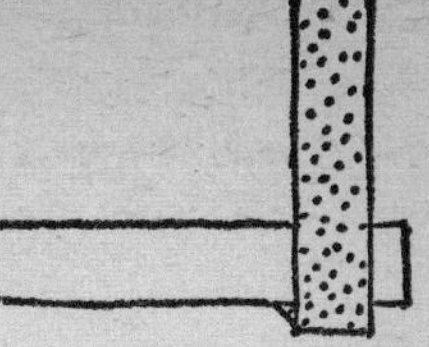

Fold the gold strip to the right:

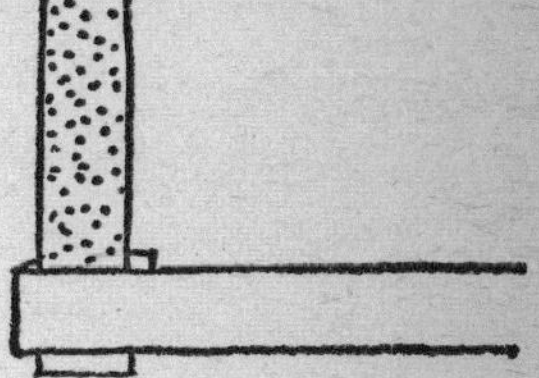

Then: red down, gold left; red up, gold right – and so on.

Finish with a dab of glue and pull out.

If you want 6′ of trimming, you will need two 12′ strips – or eight 3′ ones joined as you go along.

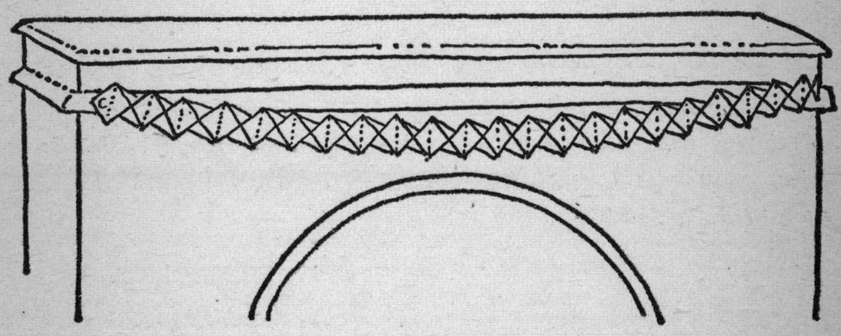

Fringe

For a fringe to put round the mantelpiece, you need a 2″ wide strip of strong paper (coloured sugar-paper would be ideal, stationers and art shops sell it), a crochet hook and some coloured raffia or wool.

Make holes in the paper, ½″ apart, with a skewer; big enough for the hook and raffia to pass through. Cut up the raffia into pieces about a foot long.

Push the hook through a hole, put a piece of raffia (folded in half) on it, and pull the raffia back through the hole.

With the loop of raffia still round the stem of the crochet hook, pull its ends up through the loop.

When the whole length is done, you can tie the lengths of raffia together as shown below.

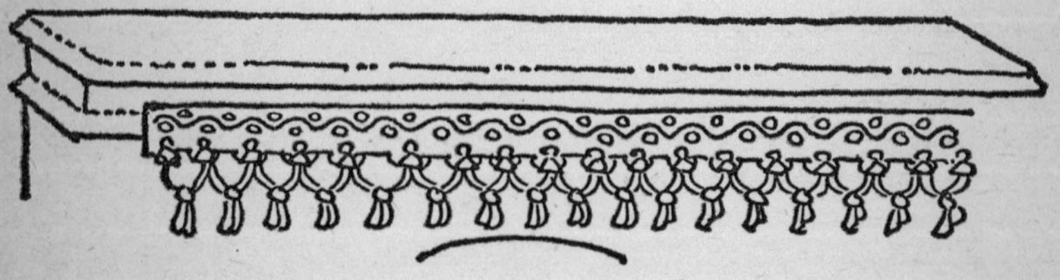

Paper chains

You can make decorative paper chains to festoon along the mantelpiece, using needle and invisible thread – or ordinary cotton – with lots of strips of coloured paper. The strips should be about 1″ wide. Their length can vary.

Using 6″ strips threaded onto the cotton, you could make chains like these:

Or you could have some strips 6″ and some 9″ long.

By glueing the ends of strips together to make circles, you could create chains like these:

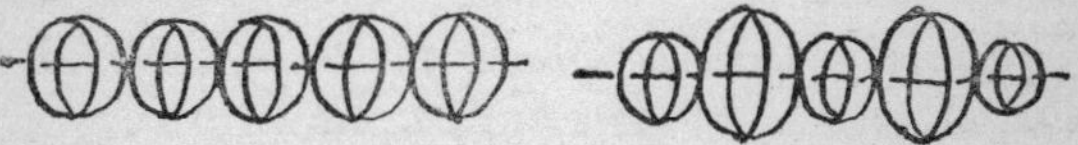

With one very long continuous strip, make these chains:

You could mix strips for even more elaborate effects:

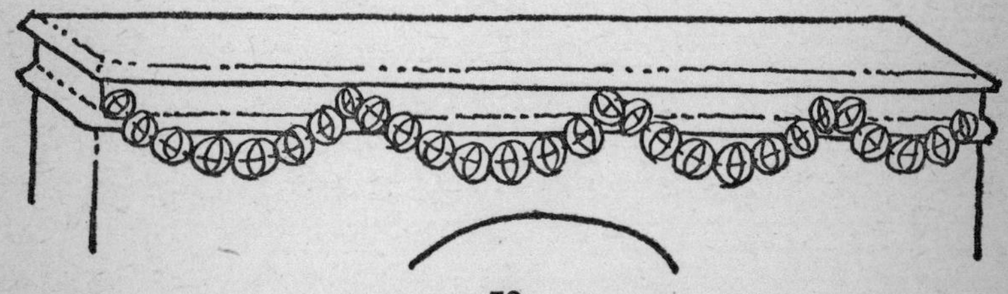

Mantelpiece Ornaments

Arcade of lanterns

For this you need either cream or yoghurt pots (painted) or little foil patty-pans, half-filled with clay, cement or any modelling material (see page 10), and some pieces of wire 18″ long.

Put the pots in a row along the mantelpiece and stick arches of wire between each. Twine the wire with tinsel or ivy, and hang lanterns between (see below) – or Christmas tree baubles.

To make each lantern, take a piece of paper preferably gold, silver or some other bright colour about 6″ by 3″ and fold in half lengthways. Snip along it like this:

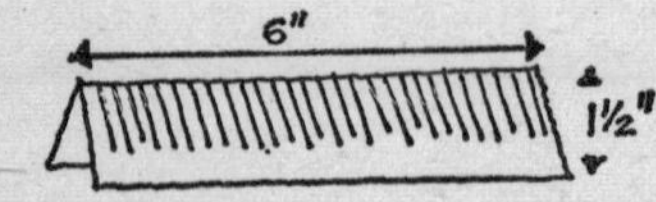

Open out and glue the ends, then glue a little paper strip over the top to hang it up:

Another way: snip the paper (*not* folded) like this:

Along the cut ends, stick a strip of paper. Then glue the ends, press into shape, and add the handles as before.

Bridge of candles

For this decoration you need to glue kitchen foil over both sides of a big piece of cardboard before cutting it out. The foil not only looks pretty but is necessary to make the card flame-proof.

Cut the cardboard into two strips about 4″ wide and as long as you like. Mark out a series of arches along one side of each, about 1½″ apart, and cut them out. (The best way is to cut one arch shape from card and draw round this.)

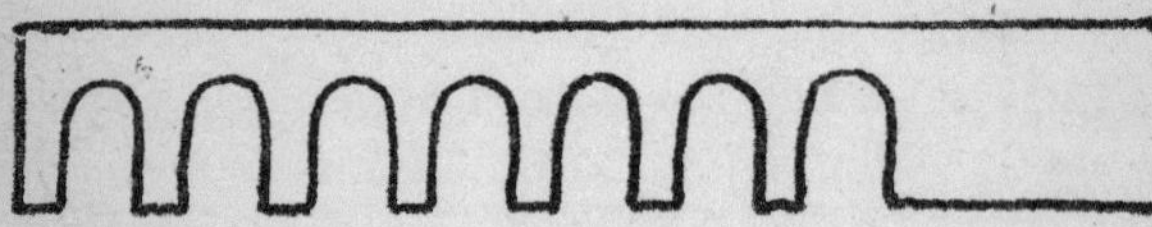

Join the two pieces by putting several 1″ card strips (8″ long) between the arches, fitting them like this:

Cover the tops of these strips with foil for safety. Then put a short candle on each, and stand the bridge on a piece of foil to catch drips of wax. (A little melted wax will hold the bottom of each candle firm.)

You could decorate the front by glueing on sparkly beads or fruit gums for a jewelled look.

Clock pavilion

For a festive occasion you can give the clock a splendid new case, made from thick paper. The size depends on the size of the clock. Measure its height and width, and write down whichever of the two is bigger. All the measurements marked X on the diagram below should be 1″ larger than this.

Cut the walls out like this (the dotted lines are folds).

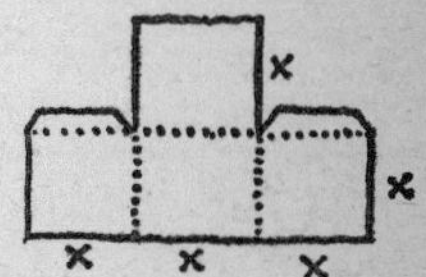

Cut a door, and decorate the walls. Be sure the clock face will show clearly through the door.

Cut the roof like this, and decorate it.

Fold the walls, and glue together by the two tabs:

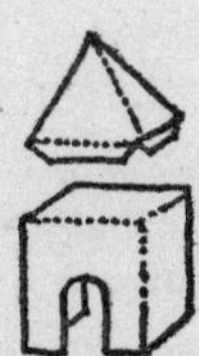

Then fold the roof, glue the tabs, and glue onto the walls.

Put over the clock.

Christmas Figures

The mantelpiece is a good place to display a scene with Christmas characters. Here are some ways of making them. Use cotton-wool snow and small branches of fir to make a wintry background.

Robins (or Easter chicks)

(1) Paint the body of the robin on some card (about 4″×2″) and cut it out.

For legs, cut and fold another card (4″×1″) like this:

Put the body into the slits.

(You can make four-legged animals like this, too – using two stands for legs. The stands are also useful for card Christmas trees, Santa, etc.)

(2) You can model birds and animals from this mixture: 1 cup salt, $\frac{1}{2}$ cup cornflour, $\frac{3}{4}$ cup water. Mix it in a bowl, put it over a saucepan of boiling water, stir till stiff (a few minutes), model your bird and leave it to cool. Use wire loops or pipecleaners for birds' legs. When dry the birds can be painted. Or use one of the modelling materials described on page 10.

Santa's reindeer (or cattle for a crib)

For the body of each one you will need a cardboard tube from a toilet roll, or else a strip of card roughly $1\frac{1}{2}''$ by $12''$ folded into a zigzag.

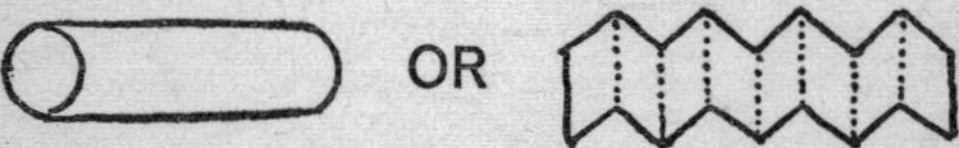

Cut two pairs of legs from cards about $4'' \times 2''$ and stick one at the front and one at the back. Glue on a tail of string or wool at the back.

Draw and cut out the head, like one of the ones below, from another card 4″×2″, to stick on the front.
Finally, paint the animal all over.

Santa's Sledge

Find or make a box about this size:

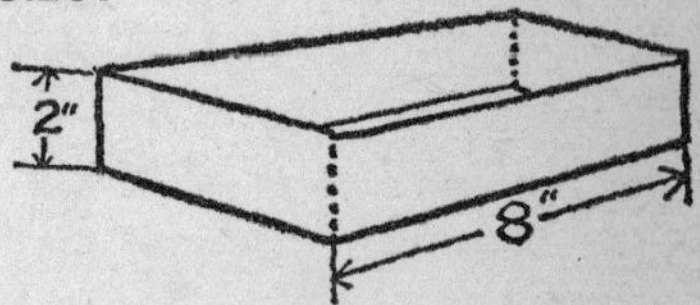

From card cut out and paint two side-pieces like this:

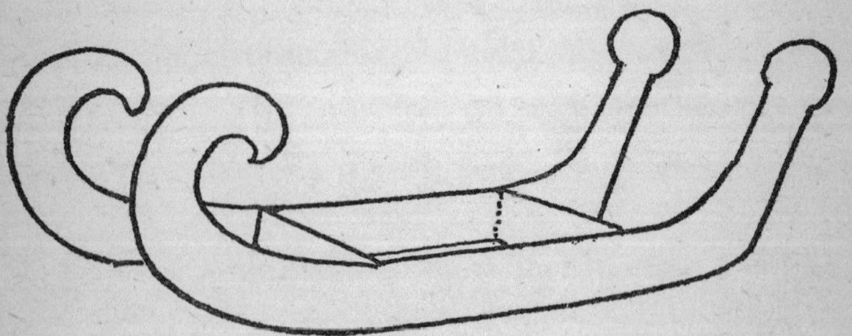

Instead of paint, you could use silver paint or glitter.
Load up the sledge with wrapped sweets, and 'harness' it to a reindeer (see p. 65) with gold or coloured string.

Festive Mural

Fasten to the wall above the fireplace enough sheets of coloured tissue to provide a big background for your work – you may need four. (Do this when the fire is not on. Use small dabs of Blu-Tack.) If you like, cut out a little background scenery and glue this on next. For example, a good bit of background scenery for a Father Christmas mural might be a silhouette (cut from black paper) of a rooftop and chimney, perhaps with a prowling black cat; and maybe a moon and stars of kitchen foil:

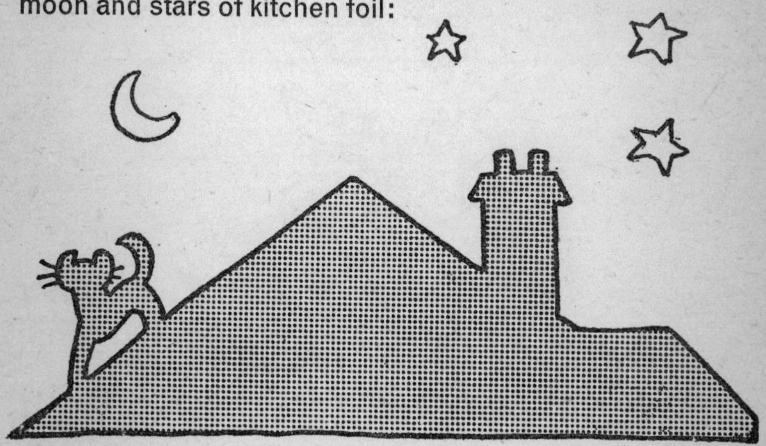

On a big sheet of white paper (or two sheets glued together) pencil the outline of your Father Christmas (or angels or any other subject you choose). Keep it big and simple, about 3′ high. Paint it in poster colours. If you like, glue glitter on, or add touches like cotton-wool 'fur'. Do whatever you fancy, but go for large, bold effects, not a lot of small detail. Then stick this onto the background with a few dabs of Copydex.

Angel Chorus

Fold up a strip of gold or coloured paper in a zigzag and cut out an angel. Be sure you don't cut all the way through the sides. Unfold and stand up.

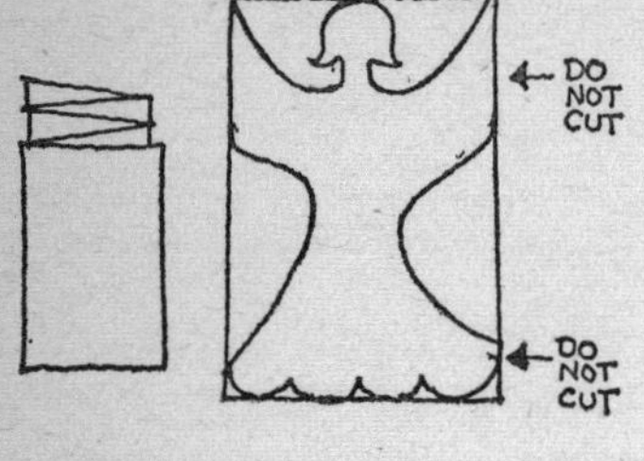

Do choirboys or carol-singers like this, too (or clowns or Easter bunnies).

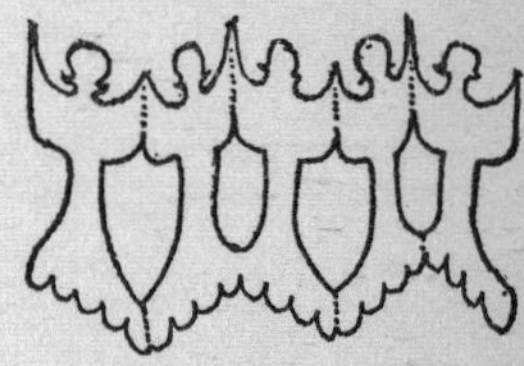

Church

Using the methods shown on pages 60–66, you can make all kinds of buildings. Here is a church:

For the cross, use wire or matchsticks. Put coloured Cellophane in the windows for stained glass (you could lay a torch inside to light them up). For snow on the roof, mix a little detergent with just enough water to make a paste. Stand on cotton-wool.

Door Decorations

Give visitors a cheery welcome as they come in, by decorating the doorway to suit the occasion.

You can trim a door-frame with edgings shown on pages 55–59. Here are some more ideas.

Festive Frieze

Either buy sheets of patterned wrapping paper to cut up into 4″ long strips, or, better still, cut up plain paper and paint your own patterns on it (or glue paper cut-outs on). Invent a design suitable to the occasion – hearts for St Valentine's day, witches for Hallowe'en, a person's initials for their birthday, eggs for Easter, and so on. If you are going to repeat the same simple shape many times, cut it out in card first and draw round it.

Round the door-frame stick a strip of double-sided Sellotape (or a trail of Copydex) and press the frieze in place. Either of these materials will come off easily afterwards, and leave no mark.

Evergreen Garlands

(1) Roll up sheets of newspaper, twisting them round as you go. Insert stems of laurel leaves or ivy so that the twists of paper hold them securely. Drawing-pin these around the top part of the door.

(2) Buy about a yard of narrow chicken-wire, and ask the shop (ironmonger or florist) to cut it in half, lengthways, for you. Curl the pieces round, with the sharp bits tucked inside. Drawing-pin round the top part of the door, then cover with short bits of holly or fir.

To either of these, you can add a few Christmas-tree baubles. You can also make circular wreaths in the same way to hang on the door.

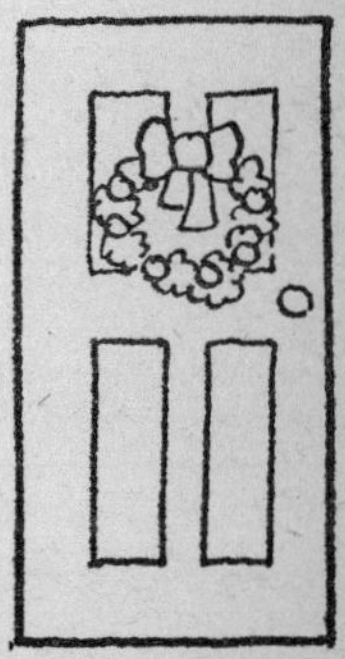

Welcome Pannier

If you put this on an outside door, make it of rainproof materials (plastic, foil, etc).

Find a cardboard box of suitable size to drawing-pin to the door. Decorate it first in any way you like – the one in the drawing is covered with felt and trimmed with fringe bought from a furnishing shop, fastened on with Copydex. Add a bow of ribbon, foil or crêpe paper. Then fill the box with leaves and gold Christmas-tree balls – or twigs and fir-cones sprayed gold – or paper flowers (see page 92) – or real flowers, with a pot of water hidden inside the box.

For other door decorations, many of the wall decorations at the beginning of this book can be used.

Light Decorations

Sparkling and transparent materials will look really festive with light shining on them.

Floodlit Tree

Instead of decorating a Christmas tree with fairy-lights, you might be able to stand it below a hanging light-bulb to shine down onto its glass baubles and glitter. For this you need to make a special shade.

Take a piece of thin card – it should be at least 15″×8″. Cover it on both sides with kitchen foil. Prick holes in it with a skewer – make up a decorative pattern. Bend it round into a tube, and glue.

Use wire to fasten this to the lamp-holder above the light bulb.

A beam of light will shine down onto the tree – or whatever else you put underneath – with little sparkles of light showing through the pricked holes.

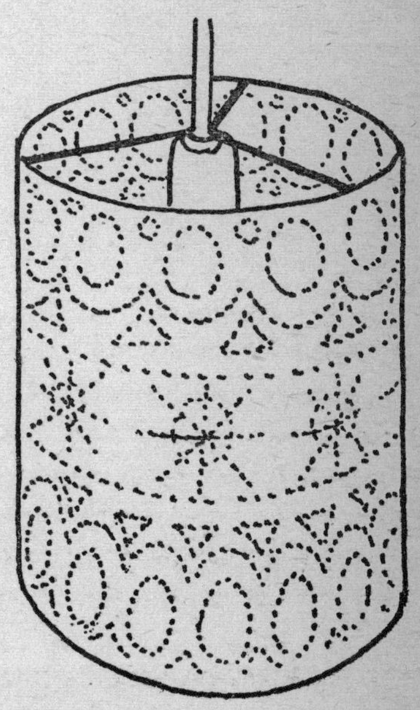

Rainbow Light

Select a lampshade, take it down ready, and then collect bits of Cellophane (or tissue) in as many different colours as you can, and several cardboard tubes (from toilet rolls, kitchen-paper rolls, etc – they need not be all the same size). Cut the tubes into 1″ lengths: a bread-knife is best for this job.

Round one edge of each bit of tube, smear some glue, and cover with a square of Cellophane.

When you have done enough to fill in the bottom of the lampshade you have chosen for your rainbow light, put them all on the table (Cellophane sides down) and run a strip of Sellotape all round to keep them together.

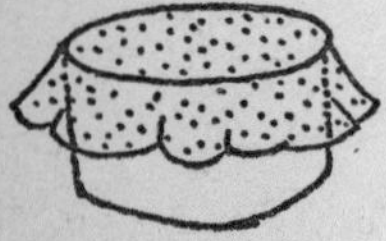

Now wedge them into the bottom of the lampshade, and they will cast a pretty pattern of coloured light downwards.

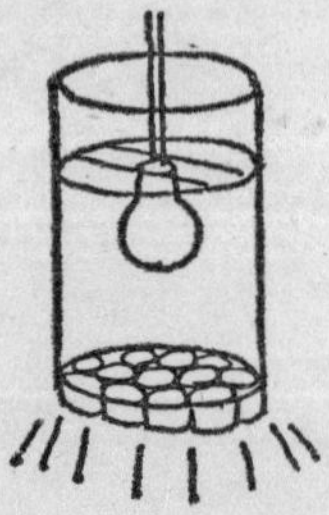

NOTE: There should be a space between the light-bulb and the card tubes. If possible, choose a dark-coloured lampshade for the best effect.

Stair Lantern

You can put this anywhere, but it looks particularly good on the post at the foot of the stairs.

Collect four foil dishes (about 6″×4″). Frozen and take-away foods are sold in them, or you can buy them in packets. Cut off the rims. You can then cut out four frames and four rectangles like this:

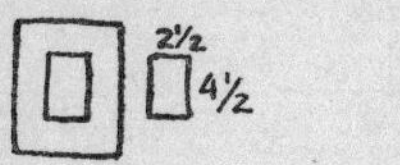

Cut and Sellotape together four foil triangles to go on top (first make a hole in each):

Put the lantern on top of the post, using Sellotape to hold it on firmly. The open side should be at the back. You can reach in through this to light a nightlight inside. Don't use a candle – it is not steady enough.

Table Decorations

Decorate the dinner-table whenever you have a party. And use small tables round the room for special little displays.

Father Christmas

This model is made to hold lots of sweets or small presents at the back. All you need is a piece of thin white card about a foot square and some shiny red paper (or use paint).

Draw this outline on the card and cut it out:

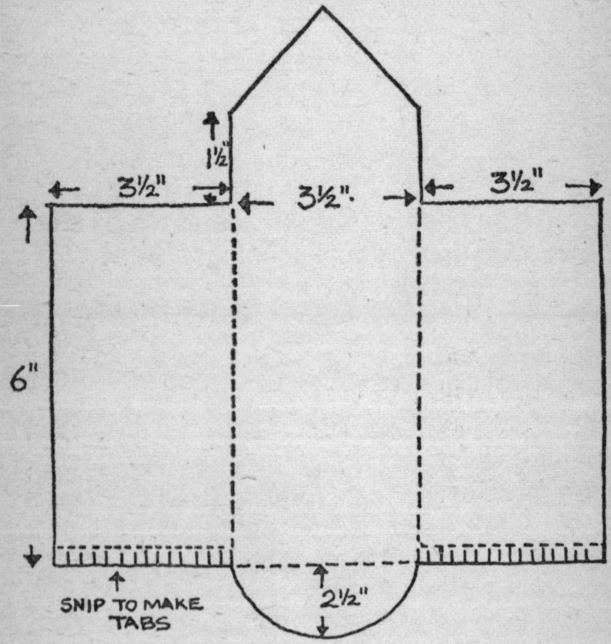

Crease along the dotted lines (it is easier to do this if you first rule a line with a knife – but don't cut right through, of course). Curve the side pieces round to the back and glue together.

The curved piece is also bent back and glued in place by means of the little tabs.

To make arms, cut two pieces of card like this, making creases along the the dotted lines:

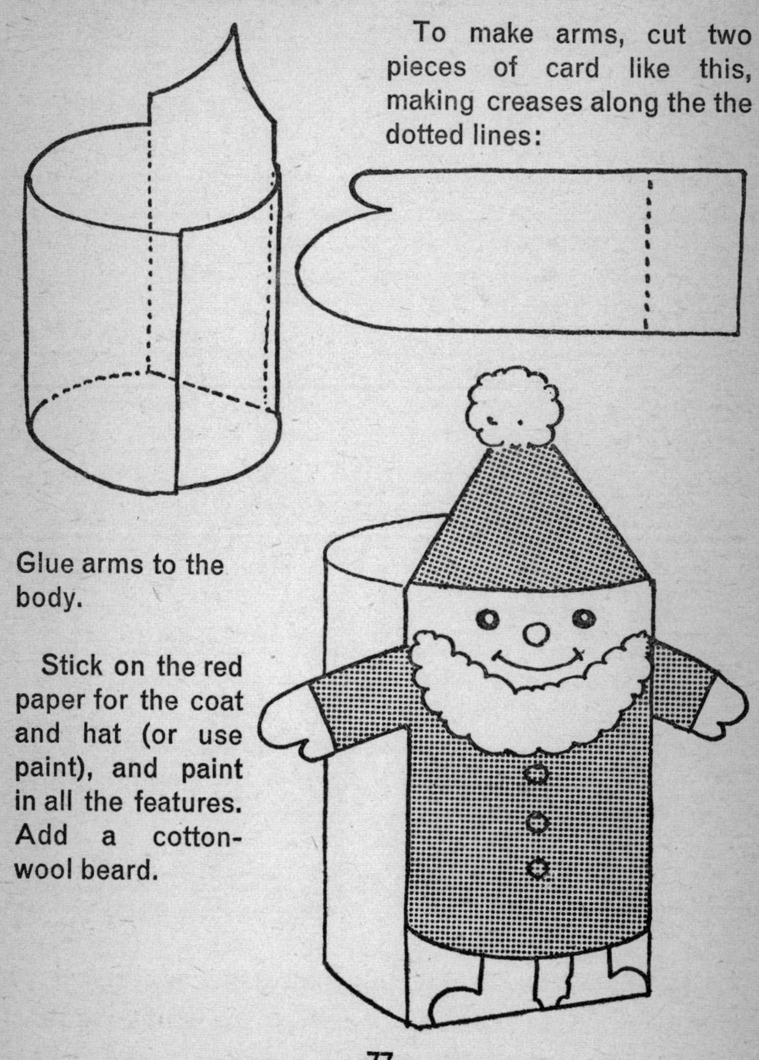

Glue arms to the body.

Stick on the red paper for the coat and hat (or use paint), and paint in all the features. Add a cotton-wool beard.

Glittering Twigs

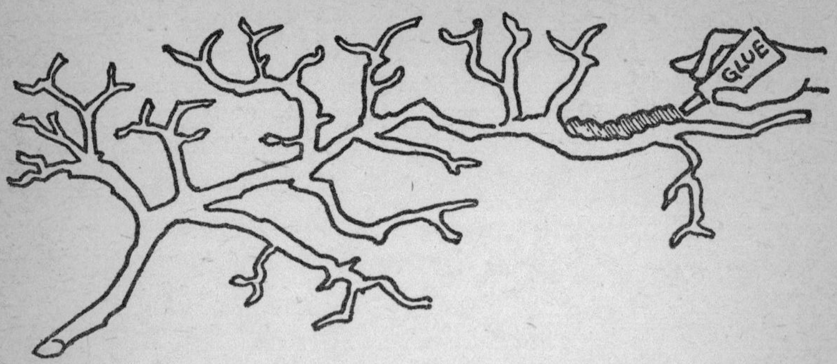

Collect some bare twigs of whatever length suits your vase and in as interesting and graceful shapes as you can find. Buy some coloured glitter. This is sold by stationers and by art shops, in various colours. You will also need a tube of glue.

Make a trail of glue along the upper surfaces of each twig, then, holding the twigs over a sheet of newspaper, sprinkle glitter on. You can hang sweets or baubles over them.

Another thing you can do with glitter: spread glue along lengths of thick wool or string, then dip in glitter, and use to make festoons on bare or white-painted twigs. Or glue the edges only of some pine cones and dip these into glitter, then pile in a bowl. Or spray them with silver or gold paint.

More Glittering Ideas

When you are having a party, at each child's place at the table put a glass or paper cup with his or her initial on it. If you are using glasses, the best adhesive is Copydex

because you can get it off afterwards. Make the outline of the initial in glue or Copydex, then drop the glitter on.

Cut a big circle of paper – large enough for the plate with the Christmas or birthday cake to go in the middle. Lightly pencil a decorative border design – then cover in glue and glitter.

Silver Fruit Basket

Ask someone for an old lampshade frame like this:

Wind strips of kitchen-foil round and round the wires. Then cut a lot of long strips about 2″ wide and roll them up. Weave these in and out of the wire uprights about an inch apart, pinching them in place. Turn the 'basket' wide side up and stand it in the middle of the table, filled with fruit (see next page).

You can use more foil strips to add decorative touches to the top.

Plait three strips together if you want a handle over the top.

A Cake Frill

You need some kitchen paper of the kind that has a patterned border on it. Cut a strip about $3\frac{1}{2}''$ wide with the pattern in the middle, and long enough to go round your cake. Now cut a matching strip of plain paper, and one of foil (or of greaseproof paper). Neatly stitch the three together, with one line of stitches down the middle. Snip the edges for a feathery effect (you can fold the frill in half to do this.)

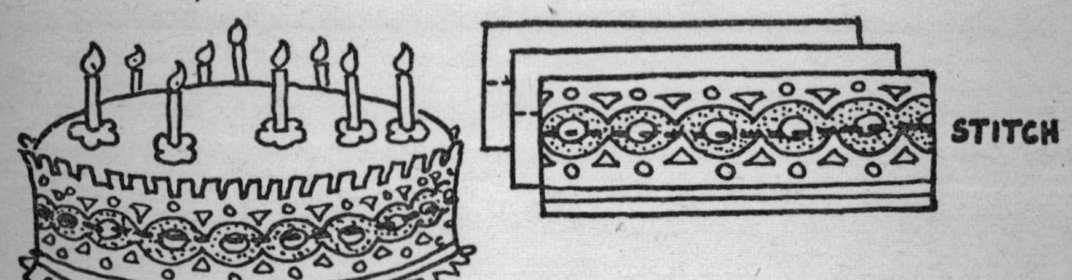

From the same roll of kitchen-paper you can make matching place-mats and napkins, and cut out strips of the pattern to decorate other things, like paper cups, fruit-squash bottles, etc.

Fun With Candles

Use an apple-corer to remove the cores from some apples and stick a candle in each one. Just right for a Hallowe'en party. (Use black candles in red apples.)

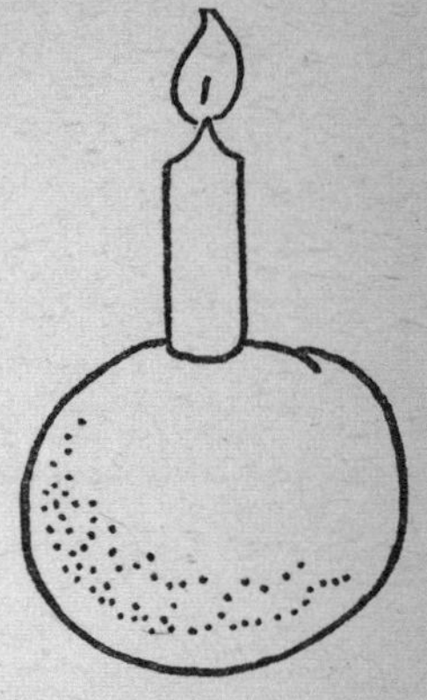

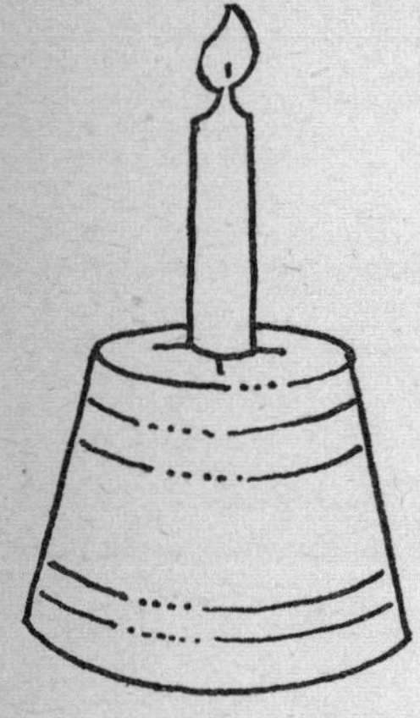

Turn some yogurt or cream pots upside down and cut a cross in the middle with a sharp knife. Cover the pots thoroughly with kitchen foil: this is important, for safety. Push a coloured candle through the cross. You could add strips of metallic Sellotape in a matching colour.

Collect dried-up leaves, nuts, seed-pods, small fir-cones etc. Spray them gold (use an aerosol can of paint) then stick a fat candle to a saucer, using a little melted wax, and arrange them around it.

Cover lots of small sea-shells with foil, pressing it smoothly over so that the markings of the shells show clearly. Use clay or any modelling material as a base. Into a lump of it, press the candle and then all the sea-shells around the bottom.

On to a small block of wood, or a firm cardboard box, glue an arrangement of nuts, fir-cones or sea-shells – use Copydex to stick them on. Add a candle, and a bow made from parcel-ribbon. Now spray *everything* gold, including the candle (use an aerosol can of paint). You could make lots of these and give them as Christmas presents.

Beside each child's place at the table put a little candle (the size that is sold for Christmas trees). Fill a foil cake-case with any kind of modelling dough and stick the candle in it. When set, coat the surface with glitter or with artificial snow (detergent mixed with just a little water.)

Fun with Flowers

Either use real flowers or, in winter, make some yourself (see page 92).

Use thin card (either sprayed gold or with gold paper glued to it) and a round cake-tin to go inside. Cut this shape from the card:

Its size depends on the size of your cake-tin. Bend round and glue. Add fruit-gums for jewels, and cotton-wool with dabs of black paint for ermine round the bottom. Put the cake-tin inside and arrange the flowers in it, then pour water in.

Put a little posy beside each person's place at the table. Take a small paper doily, fold it in four, cut the corner off and cut one quarter out. Fold round, glue, put into a wine glass, and arrange flowers inside. (Below, left.)

For Easter, use egg shells (plain or painted). A dab of Plasticine underneath will hold them firm. Fill with primroses, snowdrops, violets and other tiny flowers and leaves. (Above, right.)

Find three round tin-lids (or shallow baking tins) of different sizes, and two glasses. Decorate the edges of the lids with coloured metallic Sellotape. Pile them up like this:

Pour water into the tins, then fill with flowers. Try to find some that will trail over the edges. You could put a candle at the top.

Fix (with Copydex or Sellotape) a small bowl to the top of a tall candlestick. A foil patty-pan would do. Fill with flowers, including some trailing ones.

Party Pieces

Here are ways to give every child something personal when they sit down at the table.

Place Mats
Make these from paper – about 12″×8″. Paint a different design for each child.

Buy transparent self-adhesive plastic (Fablon or Con-Tact) and press it on; then cut out the animal shapes.

Drinks

On 2″ discs of card, paste coloured pictures or differently patterned papers. Then make two little slits.

Through each disc, push a drinking straw. Then each child will know which drink is his.

Place markers

Collect lots of huge pebbles and wash them well. When dry, paint the children's initials on decoratively, and mark each place with one. (Use poster paint.) If you like, you can varnish when the paint is dry.

Spires with secrets

Cut out the shape shown in thin card: it consists of three triangles, 3″×9″, and a tab (the shaded part). Fold the three triangles up and use the tab to glue them together. (You could first cover the card with colourful paper, or paint it, or spray it gold).

Stand one at each place – hiding a little present inside. If you like, add a flag (paper on a cocktail stick) with the child's name.

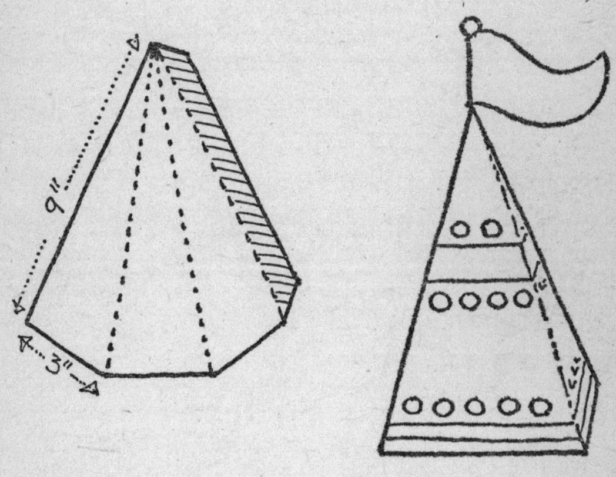

Christmas Crib

Model the figures from clay. Keep them rather dumpy, because thin bits of clay tend to break later. Leave for some days to dry (don't put near heat), then paint. Use poster paint. You can varnish this later if you want a shiny look.

Trees Use bare twigs, with a lump of clay or Plasticine to hold them.
Star of Bethlehem Cut it out of kitchen foil and hang it in a tree.
Snow Detergent mixed with very little water, or cotton wool.
Straw Cut some grass and dry it.
The stable Cut these pieces from card (the size should be suitable for the clay figures):

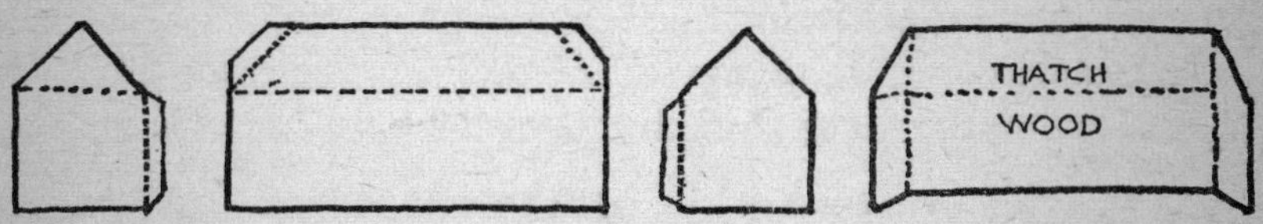

Paint to look like wood and thatch. Glue together by the tabs, creasing at the dotted lines.

Yule Log

Find a suitable log about 8″ long. Using a little melted wax, stick on some red candles – the size sold to put on Christmas trees. Spread artificial snow (detergent with a little water, or cotton wool) over the top of the log. Now use your imagination about the rest of the decoration: you could add any of the things from the following list:

- Sprigs of evergreen
- Small glass Christmas-tree baubles
- A little holly
- Dry leaves painted white
- Dry cow-parsley or other plants, covered in glitter
- Red glacé cherries
- Small foil flowers
- A bow of gold parcel-ribbon
- Trails of ivy
- Thistle-heads or fir-cones, sprayed gold

Hold them on with small pieces of Plasticine if they look insecure.

Easter Nest

Collect a lot of moss from the garden or a wood, and pack it round the edges of a small saucer. It should be as damp as possible. Poke little holes here and there and push in some small flowers, such as primroses. Then fill the centre with little foil-covered Easter eggs – the chocolate cream kind.

If you want a hen to sit on top, try this, in paper (painted). The body is a circle folded in half.

Tissue Paper Flowers

(1)

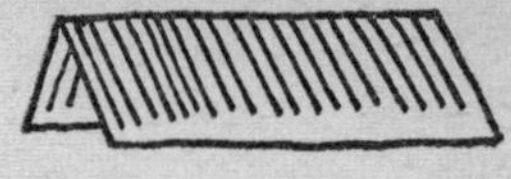

Fold and snip ($\frac{1}{2}''$ apart). Turn inside out

Roll round and Sellotape the stem. Push wire through middle

ROSE

(2)

Fold and snip ($\frac{1}{4}''$ apart). Turn inside out

Roll round and Sellotape the stem

CORNFLOWER

(3)

Cut three circles

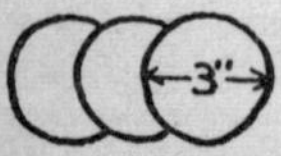

3″

Snip

Put on top of one another, arranged so that snips do not lie on top of one another

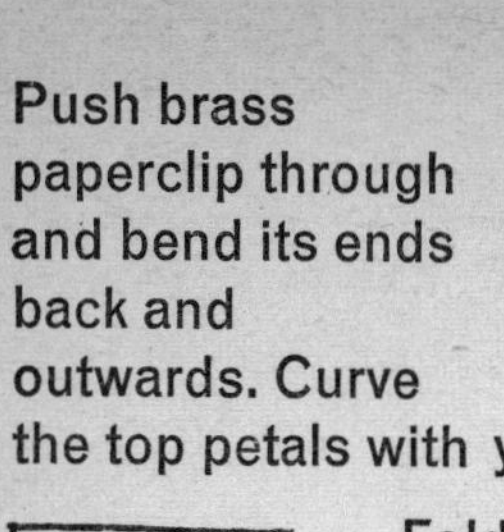

Push brass paperclip through and bend its ends back and outwards. Curve the top petals with your fingers

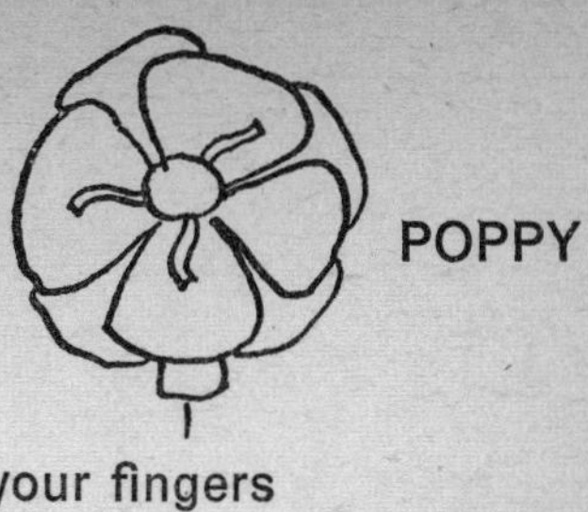

POPPY

(4) Fold in eight and cut as shown

Unfold and roll up

Pinch the bottom, Sellotape it, and pull the petals outwards.

LILY

(5) 3"

Fold in half

Curl into a cone and Sellotape

BLUEBELL

Mount several on wire.

MAKE LEAVES FROM FIRMER PAPER

Snowmen

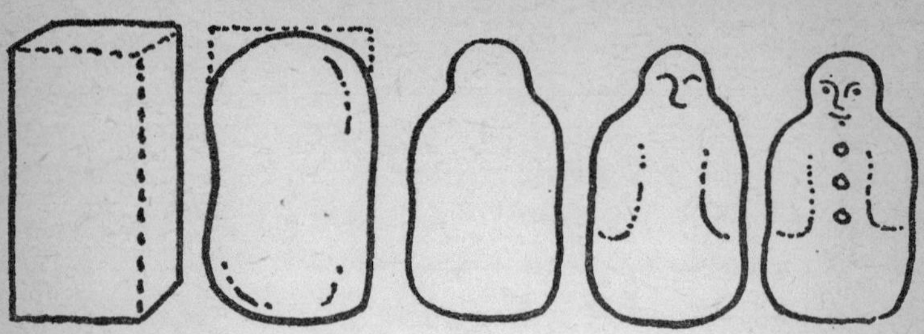

Some grocers sell cooking salt in a block. You can carve a snowman out of this. Spread plenty of newspaper around. Use an old, blunt knife and, to round off sharp angles, a bit of sandpaper.

Carve away bit by bit, removing the parts you don't need. To get the shape of the arms and nose, you may need a large nail or knitting needle. Keep turning the model round to see the sides and back. Paint features on.

Another method. Using cold-water paste, cover a plastic squeezy-bottle with strips of newspaper in many layers and, finally, with strips of white tissue to give a smooth surface.

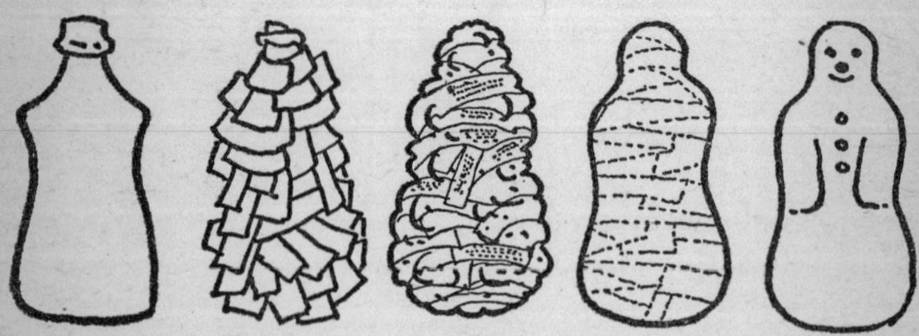

When this is dry, paint on features. For a top-hat and scarf use paper (painted).
To make the hat:

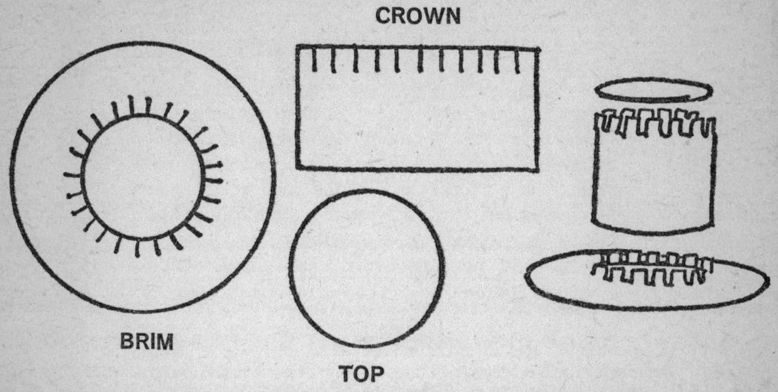

(Sizes depend on the size of your snowman's head.) Curve the crown round and glue; then, using the tabs you have snipped inside the brim, stick the two parts together. Glue the top onto the crown, using the tabs snipped at the top of the crown.

Elizabeth Gundrey